be

ANGRY

be ANGRY

His Holiness the Dalai Lama

as told to Noriyuki Ueda

HAMPTON ROADS

Hampton Roads Publishing Company, Inc.
Charlottesville, VA 22906

Distributed by Red Wheel/Weiser, LLC
www.redwheelweiser.com
Sign up for our newsletter and special offers by going to
www.redwheelweiser.com/newsletter.

Graphic image of the Dalai Lama from *www.vectorportal.com*

ISBN: 978-1-64297-007-4

Library of Congress Cataloging-in-Publication Data available upon request.

Printed in Canada

FR

10 9 8 7 6 5 4 3 2 1

Publisher's note:

It seems antithetical to use "angry" and "Dalai Lama" in the same sentence, much less the same book. After all, the Dalai Lama's life-long teaching is about the cultivation of love and compassion. But however much the Dalai Lama has to say about *avoiding* anger, he also recognizes that it is an inevitable part of the human condition. The Dalai Lama has observed: "Generally speaking, if a human being never shows anger, then I think something's wrong. He's not right in the brain."

Anger that is unrecognized and suppressed will destroy us from the inside out. But there is such a thing as wrathful compassion—an anger that is used not for one's own self-righteousness but rather seeks to protect others from harm.

In today's world, there is a lot to be angry about: injustice, social and economic inequality, racism, ignorance.

This little book is here to tell you: "Be angry."

Once we can recognize anger—how we hold it, how we manifest it, how we act upon it—then we can transform that anger to compassionate action. Only then can we bring love, peace, and healing to the world.

This book was compiled from an interview with the Dalai Lama conducted by Noriyuki Ueda, a well-known Japanese author, lecturer, and cultural anthropologist. As a visiting research fellow at the Center for Buddhist Studies at Stanford University, he taught a twenty-part lecture series on contemporary Buddhism during which his students questioned him: "Can buddhism respond to contemporary problems?"

His interview with the Dalai Lama provides insight into the answer.

ANGER

In the real world, exploitation exists, and there is a great and unjust gap between rich and poor. The question is, from a Buddhist perspective, how should we deal with inequality and social injustice? Is it un-Buddhist to feel anger and indignation in the midst of such circumstances?

This is an interesting question. Let's begin by looking at the matter first from a secular point of view—education. What do we teach about anger?

I often say we should have more serious discussion and research about whether or not our so-called modern education system is adequate enough to develop a healthier society.

Some American scientists I know are seriously concerned about social problems. Over the years, we have had many discussions about the value of compassion, and several of these scientists conducted an experiment with university students.

For a period of two to three weeks, they had the students practice attentive, deliberate meditation (mindfulness), and after the two or three weeks of meditation, the scientists investigated what changes had taken place in their subjects. They reported that after this period of meditation practice, the students became calmer, had greater mental acuity and less stress, and had increased power of memory.

The University of British Columbia in Canada has created a new institution that is conducting research on how to cultivate warm-heartedness in students within the modern educational system. At least four or five universities in the United States are acknowledging that modern education lacks something in this regard.

Research is finally being conducted to address this problem and propose ways to improve the system.

Unless there is a worldwide movement to improve education and give more attention to ethics, this work will take a very long time, and it will be very difficult.

Of course, in Russia and China the same dangers exist, and in India, too. India may be a little better off because of its heritage of traditional spiritual values, even if they probably do not think about this question in terms of logic or reason.

Japan is a modernized country and therefore Westernized, so Western problems are also occurring in Japan. With the adoption of a modern educational system, traditional values and family values have suffered. In the West, the power of the Church and its support for the family has declined, and society has suffered the consequences. In Japan, too, the influence of religious institutions has faded, and with it, families have suffered.

Now let's talk about what role religious people can play in solving social problems. All religious institutions have the same basic values—compassion, love, forgiveness, tolerance. They express and cultivate these values in different ways. And religions that accept the existence of God take a different approach from those, like Buddhism, that don't. The current pope is a very sophisticated theologian, and though he is a religious leader, he emphasizes that faith and reason must coexist.

Religion based on faith alone can end up as mysticism, but reason gives faith a foundation and makes it relevant in daily life.

In Buddhism, from the start, faith and reason must always go together. Without reason, it is just blind faith, which the Buddha rejected. Our faith must be based on the Buddha's teachings.

The Buddha first taught the Four Noble Truths, the basis of all Buddhist doctrine, according to which the law of cause and effect governs all things.

He rejected the idea of a god as creator of all things. Buddhism begins with the logical understanding that all happiness and

"BUDDHISM BEGINS WITH THE LOGICAL UNDERSTANDING THAT ALL HAPPINESS AND SUFFERING ARISES FROM SPECIFIC CAUSES."

suffering arises from specific causes. So Buddhism is rational from the start, particularly the schools of Buddhism based on the Sanskrit tradition, including Japanese Buddhism—that is, the Buddhism that carries on the great Nalanda University tradition from ancient India.

According to the Nalanda tradition, everything should be understood according to reason. We must first be skeptical and doubt everything, as we do in the modern world. Skepticism produces questions, questions lead to investigation, and investigation and experimentation bring answers.

Buddhists do not believe the teachings of the Buddha merely because he expounded them. We approach the teachings with a skeptical attitude, and then we investigate whether they are true. Once we know that a teaching is truly correct, then we can accept it.

Buddhist teachings are not mere mysticism; they are based on reason.

Japanese Buddhism has diverged considerably from that reason-based approach. For example, in Zen Buddhism, the goal is to transcend verbal logic. In the Nembutsu faith [of the Pure Land sects], the goal is to entrust ourselves completely to the saving power of Amida Buddha.

"SKEPTICISM PRODUCES QUESTIONS, QUESTIONS LEAD TO INVESTIGATION, AND INVESTIGATION AND EXPERIMENTATION BRING ANSWERS."

Because Japanese Buddhists emphasize transcending logic and surrendering oneself, they tend to say that logical statements are not really Buddhist and assume that people who think in a logical way have achieved only a low level of Buddhist understanding or have not yet completely surrendered themselves.

When these Buddhists say things like, "Don't confuse yourself with logic. Just have faith," that gives monks an excuse to stop investigating their own experience in a rational way.

Buddhism begins with our own questions, and its core is the investigation of those questions.

Often among Buddhists, when you raise your own questions, people say that you don't have sufficient faith or that you haven't practiced Buddhism enough yet.

As a result, many monks abandon the effort of thinking for themselves. To surrender oneself to the teachings of a sect's founder and believe in them absolutely, without doubting them, might at first appear to be an act that comes from a deeper faith-mind, but that act always contains the possibility of what we call blind faith.

Not only that, but the blindly faithful end up discouraging young people who seek to investigate things for themselves.

"BUDDHISM BEGINS WITH OUR OWN QUESTIONS, AND ITS CORE IS THE INVESTIGATION OF THOSE QUESTIONS."

Because young people today doubt traditional teachings, because they ask serious questions and seek to deeply investigate them, traditional Buddhism can offer them wisdom. If those questions are disregarded from the start, then the opportunity to deeply investigate Buddhist teaching is lost, and Buddhism can never become relevant for our time.

Ritual and Meaning

In Japanese temples and in many Tibetan monastic institutions, the monks perform rituals without knowing anything about their meaning, and they have no desire to study Buddhist doctrine. The ritual is just a means to earn money. They are not concerned about nirvana or the next life. They only think about how to earn money in this life. If people make offerings, the monks are happy. The same situation also exists in China and in many Christian churches around the world.

In Tibet, in some monasteries, monks who don't study are always performing rituals without knowing the meaning of the sutras. That

"IF WE ONLY PRACTICE BUDDHISM

AT THE LEVEL OF RITUAL,

IT CAN NEVER HELP US SOLVE

TODAY'S SOCIAL PROBLEMS."

is why, ever since I went into exile in India, I have said over and over again that we must study the sutras. Whether we are Tibetan, Chinese, or Japanese, we should become Buddhists of the 21st century. If we accept our religion, we must understand its meaning. Then we become serious about our faith and practice. Otherwise it's just fashion.

Since my first visit to Japan in the 1960s, I have gotten the impression that monks perform many rituals but do not pay much attention to studying Buddhist doctrine. University professors and scholars are the ones with the knowledge. Whether they are Buddhists or not, they have much more knowledge.

Fortunately, among Tibetan monks there are real scholars who possess broad and deep knowledge that comes from thirty years of study. People with blind faith will go to a temple when someone dies, and a monk will recite sutras. But if we only practice Buddhism at the level of ritual, it can never help us to solve today's social problems.

Buddhism as "Science of Mind"

The most important thing is to promote through education human values as the foundation of daily life.

I also think it is important not to think of Buddhism as a religion but as a "science of mind." Then it has greater potential to help promote basic human values.

As a science of mind, Buddhist knowledge can be used to enhance secular education and thus help students develop the qualities of affection and kindness that human beings originally possess.

"WHEN A BUDDHIST SEES POVERTY OR INJUSTICE, HE SHOULD NOT REMAIN INDIFFERENT."

In the West, scientists are now beginning to make use of Buddhist techniques—not as a religion but as a set of scientific techniques, such as meditation and the analysis of mind.

Traditionally, Buddhism is divided into so-called Hinayāna ["Small Vehicle"] and Mahāyāna ["Great Vehicle"]. Hinayāna doctrine teaches us not to harm other living beings; Mahāyāna emphasizes not only not harming others but also helping them. Therefore, when a Buddhist sees poverty or injustice, he should not remain indifferent.

In the Catholic Church in Latin America, some leaders are very concerned about social injustice, so they are leftists in that sense.

When religious people get too involved in social activism, their work becomes political. What about in Sri Lanka? Japan? I have heard that in Korea some monks are quite active in the political realm. I don't know the details, but that's what I've heard.

I think the debate is still unfolding about liberation theology, the Church's political activities in Latin America on behalf of weak members of society. Either way, it is a great effort that we cannot ignore.

In Sri Lanka, too, some monks get involved in politics. But in the ongoing civil war between the many Sinhala Buddhist sects and the few Tamil Hindu sects, political action can lead to

Buddhism being linked to Sinhalese nationalism, so it's a difficult problem.

In any case, Hinayāna Buddhism is criticized as the "Small Vehicle" that makes individual liberation its goal and is focused on self-benefit; while Mahāyāna Buddhism developed with an emphasis on altruistic practice for the salvation of others, so its nature is fundamentally social.

"ANGER BRINGS MORE ENERGY,

MORE DETERMINATION,

MORE FORCEFUL ACTION

TO CORRECT INJUSTICE."

Compassionate Anger

When faced with economic or any other kind of injustice, it is totally wrong for a religious person to remain indifferent. Religious people must struggle to solve these problems.

Here the issue is how to deal with anger. There are two types of anger. One type arises out of compassion; that kind of anger is useful. Anger that is motivated by compassion or a desire to correct social injustice, and does not seek to harm the other person, is a good anger that is worth having.

For example, a good parent, out of concern for a child's behavior, may use harsh words or even punish him. He may be angry with

"THE DEEP MOTIVATION

IS COMPASSION,

BUT IT TAKES ANGER

AS THE MEANS

TO ACCOMPLISH ITS ENDS."

the child, but there is no trace of any desire to hurt him.

Japanese temples often enshrine the fierce manifestation of [the Buddhist deity] Acala. But Acala has that fierce expression not out of hatred or a desire to harm sentient beings but out of concern for them, to correct their mistakes, like a parent's desire to correct a child's mistakes.

Anger brings more energy, more determination, more forceful action to correct injustice.

The deep motivation is compassion, but it takes anger as the means to accomplish its ends.

To use anger as a motivating force, should we transform it into another state, into something positive? Or should we maintain it as it is?

The answer to this question is a person's state of mind—that is, the motivation that causes the action. When we act, that act arises out of a cause that already exists in us.

If we act when our inner motivation is hatred toward another person, then that hatred expressed as anger will lead to destructive action. This is negative action. But if we act out of consideration for the other person, if we are motivated by affection and sympathy, then we can act out of anger because we are concerned for that person's well-being.

"WHEN WE ACT,
THAT ACT ARISES OUT OF
A CAUSE THAT ALREADY
EXISTS IN US."

"HATRED EXPRESSED AS ANGER WILL LEAD TO DESTRUCTIVE ACTION. COMPASSION EXPRESSED AS ANGER LEADS TO POSITIVE CHANGE."

In this way, the parent acts out of concern for the child. If a child is playing with poison, for example, there is a danger that he may put it in his mouth. That is an emergency situation, and the parent may shout or strike the child's hands, but only out of genuine concern for him, to stop him from doing something dangerous. As soon as the child drops the poison, the parent's anger stops. That is because the anger was directed toward the child's actions that could harm him, not toward the child himself. In such a case, it is right to take the necessary measures to stop the action, whether through anger, shouting, or striking.

Conversely, if the anger is directed toward the person rather than the action, if there is ill feeling toward the person, then that feeling will persist for a long time. When someone tries to harm you, or you feel that you have been harmed, then you have a negative feeling toward that person, and even if he is no longer acting in that way, you still feel uncomfortable toward him. In the case of the parent and child, as soon as the child's wrong action stops, the parent's anger goes away. These two types of anger are very different.

Now, what about anger toward social injustice? Does it last for a very long time, until the social injustice goes away?

Anger toward social injustice will remain until the goal is achieved. It has to remain.

In this case, one should truly continue to harbor a feeling of anger. That anger is directed toward the social injustice itself, along with the struggle to correct it, so the anger should be maintained until the goal is achieved. It is necessary in order to stop social injustice and wrong destructive actions.

For example, a negative or harsh attitude toward Chinese wrongdoing, such as human rights violations and torture, will remain so long as those actions continue. One will be angry as long as injustice remains.

"ANGER TOWARD SOCIAL INJUSTICE
WILL REMAIN UNTIL THE GOAL IS
ACHIEVED. IT HAS TO REMAIN.
ONE SHOULD TRULY CONTINUE
TO HARBOR A FEELING OF ANGER."

Good and Bad Attachments

Many of the Japanese monks I know who are engaged in various forms of social action are inspired by anger or indignation, but other monks often tell them that they are not yet enlightened and have only a low level of Buddhist insight.

Japanese Buddhism teaches that regardless of whether or not anger is based on compassion, we should suppress it. Even in the face of social injustice, even if terrible things are going on, to be angry is not Buddhist—it is an outrage against Buddhist doctrine. At the same time, many monks get angry about trivial things.

"PEOPLE OFTEN MISTAKE

DETACHMENT

FOR INDIFFERENCE."

I think we are talking about understanding anger on an intellectual level.

I once spoke to a wealthy Swiss woman who asked me about attachment. Buddhism teaches that we must overcome attachment, but people often mistake detachment for indifference. This woman thought that overcoming attachment meant not even acknowledging good things as good. For example, she asked me if the mind that seeks enlightenment is not attachment to enlightenment, and shouldn't we get rid of it? But the mind that seeks enlightenment is an attachment that we should keep, not discard. The attachment that seeks what is good is worthwhile.

This woman also said that without attachment, she could not truly engage in altruistic practice. But that is also a mistaken view. The kind of attachment that we must discard is the desire that is based on biased views. I said that bodhisattvas have many attachments. The valuable desire of an unbiased heart is not the kind of attachment that we should discard.

In Buddhism, to get rid of attachment means to get rid of misguided desires, but we still need valuable and good desires, and they should not be discarded.

Valuable and good desires, such as the mind that seeks enlightenment, are not the kind of desires that Buddhism teaches we must overcome. For the sake of realizing the good mind that has greater goals, such as enlightenment, we have to overcome the mind of attachment that has only small goals based on biased views.

This idea may be difficult to understand, since we use the word "attachment" to refer to both kinds of desire. But the mind that seeks good things such as enlightenment is worth keeping, while the mind of attachment based on biased views must be extinguished.

In theory, it is true that anger is never good, and we must get rid of all attachment. But when we actually confront social injustice and think about how to correct it, not all anger is bad, and we shouldn't try

"THE KIND OF ATTACHMENT

THAT WE MUST DISCARD

IS THE DESIRE THAT IS BASED

ON BIASED VIEWS. . . .

... THE VALUABLE DESIRE OF

AN UNBIASED HEART IS NOT

THE KIND OF ATTACHMENT

THAT WE SHOULD DISCARD."

to overcome all attachment. Anger is bad in theory, and we must get rid of attachment, but in practice, we cannot completely negate them all. We must discern between theory and practice.

Understanding these two kinds of attachment—good attachments and bad attachments—can really open our eyes. Most people are mystified by this question of attachment.

In Japanese Buddhism, a small number of very influential Zen, Shingon, and other monks have said that they are enlightened and detached from material things, so even if they have several expensive foreign cars or Rolex watches, carouse with geisha

"ANGER IS BAD IN THEORY,

AND WE MUST GET RID OF

ATTACHMENT.

BUT WE MUST DISCERN BETWEEN

THEORY AND PRACTICE."

every night, and spend incredible amounts of money, it's no problem because they are "detached."

Any ordinary person would think this discrepancy was odd. The monks use the logic of overcoming attachment in Buddhism to justify their actions. These few monks' behavior has alienated many Japanese from the Buddhist faith and has made them think it is a waste of time.

To overcome attachment does not mean to become indifferent. Bad attachment should be abandoned, but good attachment should be maintained as we keep striving to improve ourselves.

According to the Tibetan esoteric teaching of Dzogchen, when we undergo religious training, we have to have a correct knowledge of how to act and how not to act. These monks who say they don't have any more attachments are, in reality, enjoying many worldly things. They are supposed to have this inner understanding, yet they behave in a misguided way that reveals just the opposite. We have to express in practice what we have inwardly understood. They say they understand, but their actions show their understanding is false.

The practice of the precepts (Vinaya), which plays an important role in Buddhism, offers much practical advice. Zen and other

"TO OVERCOME ATTACHMENT

DOES NOT MEAN

TO BECOME INDIFFERENT."

"higher" forms of practice take mental understanding more seriously than they do physical actions in daily life, which they consider to be insignificant since these actions belong to a lower level of existence.

I think Vinaya is not practiced very much in Japanese Buddhist monasteries. The same thing happens in Tibetan society. Many senior monks living in the United States say they have attained deep enlightenment, and that since they are engaged in such a high level of religious practice, it doesn't matter what they do. So they behave just like any worldly person. Of course, in Buddhist practice, no matter what a person has inwardly understood, he must keep the precepts, and that kind of behavior is evidence that one is not practicing the precepts.

Generally, because spirituality is seen as so important, enlightenment is overemphasized, and we tend to disregard behavior in daily life because it is something that belongs to a lower level. The behavior of those monks I described says more about what kind of people they are than it does about Japanese Buddhism.

But the fact that they exist and sometimes wield considerable authority in their communities does reflect problems inherent to Japanese Buddhism.

Of course, in Japan there are also many monks who deserve sincere respect.

"BECAUSE SPIRITUALITY IS SEEN AS SO IMPORTANT, ENLIGHTENMENT IS OVEREMPHASIZED, AND WE TEND TO DISREGARD BEHAVIOR IN DAILY LIFE."

Knowledge and Practice

In Tibetan monasteries there is a tendency for monks to study the meaning of the sutras but not to calm their minds through practice. They gain knowledge but do not practice it.

Since ancient times, monks in the monasteries have studied the sutras and at the same time have been taught the system of Lamrim [or the "Great Exposition on the Stages of the Path," by Tibet's great scholar monk Tsongkhapa, 1357–1419], which focuses on calming the mind and transforming the personality. But recently our monks focus more on the sutras and less on Lamrim. It depends on the master who is teaching, but if he is a great master, he will teach not only the sutras but also good methods for calming the mind and improving oneself.

If a master offers only knowledge, then no matter how much his disciple knows about the sutras, he may still be arrogant, jealous, and ignorant, and his mind will not be quieted. Those are signs that a person has gotten caught up in study without practice.

The Buddha clearly taught that even if one has great knowledge, if his mind is not quiet, then the knowledge is worthless. Tsongkhapa composed a gatha [four-line verse] that says, "Even if one hears many teachings, if his heart is not calm, then he has not practiced them." When we receive teachings from a master, we should not accept them only on an intellectual level but must take them to heart and use them to quiet our minds. In Tibetan monasteries, monks learn not only to recite sutras but also the teachings of Lamrim, so they take the meaning of the sutras into their own hearts and use them to direct their minds in a positive way.

The Dilemma of Modernization and Faith

Until now, in traditional Buddhism, knowledge was transmitted from master to disciple, with the master paying careful attention to the each stage of the disciple's learning and spiritual growth and passing on only the knowledge and practice that were appropriate for that point in his development.

Since ancient times, Buddhist education has been passed down from master to disciple in this flexible way. In Japan, some argue that Buddhist knowledge should not be transmitted in a formal setting like a university, outside the context of a master-disciple relationship, where it may be subject to serious misinterpretation.

Some monasteries in Tibet are also becoming like universities. Some now go by the name "university." Of course, in their Buddhist studies programs they offer individual courses just as in any other university, but the difference between these institutions and ordinary universities is that their teachings usually emphasize that disciples must transform their own hearts through the teachings of Lamrim. They teach clearly which kinds of actions should be cultivated and which kinds should be overcome. These institutions may call themselves universities, but their approach sets them apart.

Tibetans in exile in India, however, go through the regular educational system, and fewer and fewer young people are now entering monasteries once they complete their secular education. Young people who come straight from Tibet and don't yet have a clear understanding of this situation probably do still enter the monasteries.

Recently many people have ended up migrating to the United States and other Western countries, and the number of monks who enter the monasteries to study Buddhism is dwindling. There is a danger that when they come out of the schools in the regular modern educational system, they will not be very interested in religion.

What will happen if Tibet becomes a modern society? Certainly fewer and fewer people will enter the monasteries.

If Tibetans adopt a modern educational system, and Tibetans' way of earning a living changes as a result, then monasteries may become mere academic institutions. That would be really dangerous for Tibetan society.

What should we do? We should put more energy into teaching Buddhism in schools. If we come up with a policy to incorporate the study of Buddhism in schools within the modern educational system as well, then those who come out of these schools will still have a knowledge of and interest in Buddhism, and some may decide to enter monasteries so that they can transform their minds. For this purpose, we must also create Buddhist universities and institutions where ordinary young laypeople, male or female, can go to study.

If they all were to enter monasteries and become monks and nuns, there would be far too many of them who should never have been there in the first place.

It is necessary to create such universities for young people who are interested in practicing Buddhism and polishing their minds as laypeople.

The Institute of Buddhist Dialectics in Dharamsala does not admit Tibetan women. This enrollment policy is now being debated, but no decision has yet been made. It should definitely be changed, so that laywomen will have a place to study Buddhism. Some Tibetan women who applied to study at the Institute of Buddhist Dialectics but were not admitted are now studying at the nunnery Jamyang Choling Institute. I have spoken with one of their teachers, the *geshe* of Loseling monastery [in South India], and I understand that these women are extremely gifted and passionate students of Buddhism. We must create institutions where women like this can study.

Of course, it would be difficult for monasteries to begin admitting laypeople, but all men and women, lay or monastic, should have places to study Buddhism. Parents who are well educated in Buddhism can pass on that knowledge and practice to their children. The Institute of Buddhist Dialectics admits foreigners, but is still closed to Tibetan laywomen.

Competition and Anger

All right. Returning again to the question of how to create an altruistic society, I want to talk about the meaning of competition.

More and more, modern society is governed by tough competition, which makes life very difficult. One problem is our desire to become this competitive society, but another problem is that those who criticize this competitiveness tend to emphasize only its negative side. But I believe that competition can also be very valuable.

I think there are two kinds of competition. First there is the kind that allows us to empower each other. For example, in martial arts such as judo and kendo, when two people compete, they are not caught up in winning or losing but battle as rivals who enhance each other's strengths, which is a great thing.

But nowadays in greater society, we have adopted a Western [American] type of competition that determines a winner and a loser. The result is that the winner takes all and the loser suffers, and no matter how difficult his life becomes he has to bear it, because he lost the competition.

This kind of competition that produces a winner and loser, a winning team and a losing team, is becoming more prevalent.

This kind of competition that creates "winners" and "losers" causes happiness and it causes anger.

I make a distinction between the good and worthwhile kind of competition and the other kind that is not. In the best kind of competition, we aim to accomplish a particular goal, and when we look at the good qualities that others possess, we want to achieve the same thing for ourselves. That kind of competition is positive.

In Buddhism we say, "Take refuge in the three treasures of the Buddha, dharma, and sangha," and in a sense we feel a kind of rivalry with the "three treasures." We take the

"COMPETITION THAT CREATES

WINNERS AND LOSERS

CAUSES HAPPINESS AND

IT CAUSES ANGER."

Buddha and sangha [monastic community] as our models, so that we can strive to attain a higher state. This kind of competition is positive and necessary for our development.

Then there is the negative type of competition that must be overcome. This is the type of competition that draws a line and says, "I am the winner, and you are the loser."

In this type of competition, we try to harm the other person and put ourselves first, and in that way we create our own enemy.

The more prevalent this type of competition becomes, the more problems it creates in a society. But a positive spirit of competition

"THE MORE PREVALENT NEGATIVE COMPETITION BECOMES, THE MORE PROBLEMS IT CREATES IN A SOCIETY."

"WHILE COMPASSION BRINGS A COMMUNITY CLOSER, ANGER DOES THE OPPOSITE."

allows us to lift each other up, to help each other, so that everybody ends up on top.

Around the globe, many kinds of competition exist. Last year I saw that, in the United States, competition is all about winning and losing. Even if I win today, I might lose tomorrow, so the harsh reality is that my mind can never rest.

China is the same way. In China, once you lose it's all over. [Makes a gesture of cutting his throat, laughs.]

The same thing is happening in Japan. Until now, competition in Japan allowed people to inspire each other. People trusted each other and society. But the competition now aspired to is the law of the jungle, the kind that determines a winning team and a losing team. This causes a lack of respect and trust in each other.

Bad competition causes trust in society to be lost.

The Buddha's Spirit of Social Service

Buddhist teachings take human suffering as their starting point, and today we must also begin by asking what kind of suffering we now face.

When monks just deliver their sermons, prepared in advance with no attention to people's actual suffering, then they may talk about Buddhism, but their way of explaining it is not Buddhist. Their approach is far removed from Śākyamuni's original desire to save people from suffering.

In the 1960s, I had the opportunity to visit Thailand several times. On one occasion,

I spoke with the supreme head of Thai monastic Buddhism, the Sangharaja, and I said to him, "Our Christian brothers and sisters work very sincerely for the good of society, in education, medicine, and welfare. We Buddhists traditionally lack those activities, but I think we should learn some of those practices from our Christian brothers and sisters."

But the Sangharaja told me, "No, we Buddhist monks should remain isolated from society."

It's true. The Vinaya sutra says that monks should remain isolated from society. But that does not mean we should avoid any useful or beneficial engagement in society.

The Vinaya says that a monk should live in a peaceful place, isolated from worldly people, keep the monastic rules, and follow a pure way of life, but that does not mean he cannot engage in service to society, including social work, welfare, or education.

The Buddha himself is a good example. One day he noticed a very sick monk whose body was dirty because no one had looked after him. So the Buddha himself brought water and poured it over him, and asked his disciple Ananda to wash the sick monk's body.

The Buddha did not only preach but also acted. That is truly social service. Like Jesus Christ, we followers of Buddha must have the same spirit of helping the sick and the poor and working on behalf of modern education.

In Thai monastic tradition, monks can live according to the Vinaya sutra, isolated from worldly life, but they should also emulate the Buddha's own charitable activities. Both aspects of religious life should be correctly understood and combined. The rule that says Buddhist monks and nuns should be isolated from worldly society does not mean that they are prohibited from doing any kind of social work.

I have heard that recently in Thailand, with its Hinayāna tradition of striving for self-liberation, a small but growing number of monks are getting involved with social action.

Beginning in the 1970s, some Thai monks started to practice social action. They are known as "development monks," and they are involved in activities like building hospices for AIDS patients and developing reciprocal aid programs for helping the poor.

I have also heard about monks involved with environmental issues. But in general I don't know much about it. In any case, our Christian brothers and sisters are much more active in social service.

Buddhist training is based on the practice of karuna, or compassion. And compassion must be implemented in the form of social service. That's very crucial.

According to Buddhism, it is not that God determines everything, but we ourselves create the world; Buddhism is a teaching that begins by strengthening individual subjectivity.

To be angry is a very subjective thing. To be angry in a positive way means we open our eyes to the suffering in the world, to social injustice.

To take refuge in the Buddha does not mean to entrust everything to the Buddha, but

"BUDDHIST TRAINING IS BASED ON THE PRACTICE OF COMPASSION. AND COMPASSION MUST BE IMPLEMENTED IN THE FORM OF SOCIAL SERVICE. THAT'S VERY CRUCIAL."

rather it means to embrace a positive spirit of rivalry with the Buddha, to declare our own determination to become Buddhas.

That act brings out the power latent in me, so that I have the pride, compassion, and kindness to improve myself and act in the world.

At times I may have compassionate anger, and I will abandon attachments that must be abandoned, but I will hold tightly to the Bodhisattva's attachment to relieving the suffering in the world.

Transcending Suffering

I would like to emphasize the importance of the middle path. The middle path is very important in Buddhism, but it does not simply mean staying in the middle, avoiding extremes.

The Buddha himself was born as a prince and enjoyed a life of worldly pleasure in the palace, and then renounced the world and went to live as an ascetic far from human civilization, where he practiced fasting and austerities until he nearly died.

Even through those ascetic practices, he did not attain enlightenment, so he came out of the forest, healed his mind and body, and then entered into meditation and attained enlightenment.

The middle path means avoiding extremes of pleasure and pain, but it does not mean that we should merely remain in the middle from the start.

Sometimes we go to the places where people are suffering to experience what they are going through firsthand, and other times we seclude ourselves quietly in a monastery.

In Buddhism, the true meaning of the middle way is moving dynamically between the two, experiencing both. Sometimes monks and Buddhists do not address the actual problem of suffering, because they mistakenly think that the middle path means just to sit comfortably in the middle, avoiding extremes, without doing anything.

Suffering should make us angry. This type of anger moves us toward a wrathful compassion to take action to end suffering.

Very often there are large gatherings of people who come together for the cause of world peace. But do we think world peace is important because the Buddha taught that it is? Or is it important because we ourselves are deeply convinced that we must do something to help the situation in the world?

It is not enough to want peace just because the Buddha taught that peace is important.

No matter how much we have personally experienced the horror of violence, unless we are convinced of the need for peace, it means nothing to go around merely repeating that the Buddha taught that peace is important. It is not enough to remain quietly meditating in the monastery—we must confront the violence in the outside world.

It is foolish to say that the middle path means to be indifferent to reality or not even to know about the other extremes.

The Buddha taught the need for peace. Naturally we may ask why he taught that peace is important.

Why?

"IT MEANS NOTHING TO GO AROUND MERELY REPEATING BUDDHA'S TEACHING THAT PEACE IS IMPORTANT—WE MUST CONFRONT THE VIOLENCE IN THE OUTSIDE WORLD."

We know that violence causes suffering. So we may seek peace because we think that to get rid of that suffering we must put an end to violence. We need to have both the Buddha's teachings and the awareness that is based on our own actual experience.

If we look at the Buddha's life story, it is clear why he taught the middle path. The Buddha himself taught based on his own experience. He started out as a young prince from a wealthy household, who was very spoiled and was not aware that after birth human beings experience old age, sickness, and death.

Blessed in every way, the Buddha never imagined that he himself would get old, get sick, and die, but when he actually went out of the palace and saw the lives of the people in the town, when he saw the sick, the old, and the dying, then for the first time he understood that reality.

He was astonished when he saw for himself people that were experiencing the suffering of birth, old age, sickness, and death, and he realized that sooner or later he, too, would experience those things.

Then, for the first time, he became aware of the reality of human suffering. He abandoned his wealthy lifestyle and his position as a prince, renounced the world, went off alone to undergo religious training, and practiced austerities for six years.

"ALL OF THE BUDDHA'S TEACHINGS ARE BASED ON HIS OWN EXPERIENCE."

During that period, he often fasted, but he ultimately realized that fasting and other physical efforts were not sufficient.

He saw that he had to use his intelligence, so he stopped his ascetic practices and began to eat again.

When he used his intelligence to cultivate wisdom, then, for the first time, he attained enlightenment.

All of the Buddha's teachings are based on his own experience. First, we must become aware of suffering. Even without trying to, sooner or later we all experience suffering and want to put an end to it.

To eliminate suffering, we must understand that ascetic physical practices are not enough but that it is absolutely essential to use our human intelligence to cultivate wisdom. The Buddha himself taught based on his own experience, and we too must start with our own experience of suffering.

Other religious leaders say the same thing. For example, Jesus Christ went through many difficulties and suffered terribly, and in the end he was crucified.

But I think the teaching of Buddhism is more precise and more human in its approach to suffering.

Cultivating Compassion

Now let us return to the original question about how to build an altruistic society in today's world. Can we be angry? Is it un-Buddhist to be angry?

Let's look at Japanese society. Japanese leaders and the population in general are well educated and have considerable material wealth. In that state, naturally they may not pay much attention to the importance of deeper human values.

Schools bear the responsibility for educating young people, but they do not do much to cultivate these values. From kindergarten through university, the intellectual aspects of education are treated as important, but the educational system never concerns itself with these deeper values.

Cultivating these values is supposed to be the job of religion, but religion has become so caught up in making money that it has become superficial.

The Buddha taught about the importance of compassion, but even though monks study these teachings, often they are not serious about what they are doing. They stop at an intellectual level and do not really practice what they have learned.

I feel that our modern educational system fails to provide sufficient education about compassion.

The time has come to transform this whole system. Society is formed through its educational system, but the educational system does not transmit the deeper human values of compassion and kindness.

Then all of society lives with this false view that leads to a superficial life in which we live like machines that don't need affection. We become part of that. We become like machines.

That is because today's society is based on money. A society that is based on money is

"A SOCIETY THAT IS BASED ON MONEY IS AGGRESSIVE, AND THOSE WITH POWER CAN BULLY AND BEHAVE CRUELLY TO OTHERS. . . .

...THIS SITUATION PRODUCES

GROWING SOCIAL UNREST."

aggressive, and those with power can bully and behave cruelly to others. This situation produces growing social unrest. A society that depends on money has problems that reflect its beliefs.

In reality, affection and compassion have no direct link with money. They cannot create money. Therefore, in a society in which money is the priority, people don't take these values seriously anymore.

People in positions of leadership, like politicians, have emerged from within a society that depends on money, so naturally they think like that and lead society further in that direction.

In this kind of society, people who value affection and compassion are treated like fools, while those whose priority is making money become more and more arrogant.

To be angry *on behalf* of those who are treated unjustly means that we have compassionate anger. This type of anger leads to right action, and leads to social change.

To be angry *toward* the people in power does not create change. It creates more anger, more resentment, more fighting.

Faith and Social Development

In a community that is filled with affection and kindness, even if people are materially poor, they can be happy. For example, even though many villages in Sri Lanka are materially poor, people help each other and share in each other's lives, and I have seen many examples of how they live happily in spite of their poverty.

Compare this to Silicon Valley in California, where many wealthy people live. Yet in spite of their apparent wealth, people there don't seem to be truly happy. Many suffer from stress and anxiety.

Today they may have a lot of money, but they worry about tomorrow—they fear going bankrupt or broke, and they face the stress and frustration of living on a tight schedule.

This reality raises complicated questions. Material wealth does not necessarily bring true happiness. On the other hand, while it is good to be happy in the midst of poverty, poor countries have big social problems.

On a macro scale, we must bridge the gap between rich and poor.

Buddhists with deep faith seem happy within their communities, yet in the wider world that gap keeps getting bigger.

"TO BE ANGRY <u>ON BEHALF</u>

OF THOSE WHO ARE TREATED

UNJUSTLY MEANS THAT WE HAVE

COMPASSIONATE ANGER."

"TO BE ANGRY <u>TOWARD</u> THE

PEOPLE IN POWER

DOES NOT CREATE CHANGE.

IT CREATES MORE ANGER."

People who are filled with affection and kindness, who are *not* swept away by material desires, are getting poorer; while those who are frustrated and recklessly pursue selfish benefits instead are getting richer.

What should we think of that?

What I'm going to say now is not based on serious research but is just something I thought up in my mind.

Looking back at history, my rough impression is that in European countries around a thousand years ago, people's lives were very difficult. In countries with warm climates like Africa, India, China, and other parts of Asia, fruits and vegetables were available all year round. But European countries to the north had snow in the winter, so crops could only be grown in the summer, which made life extremely difficult.

Northern countries were also probably better off in ancient times, but as their populations gradually increased—in countries with little land area, like England, for example—living conditions became increasingly difficult. So they had to think about how to get more food from other lands.

In the case of England, since it is a small island nation, food had to be brought by boat from other places. And then to acquire resources from these countries, they needed weapons.

The warmer Asian countries had relatively small populations, and because of their climates, food was available all year round. So they had no need to acquire resources from other countries.

Europeans were forced to create technology because of their difficult climate conditions. They had to think about industrialization and technology in order to survive. Countries like Portugal, Spain, England, France, and Belgium became colonial powers. These small countries became industrialized, obtained raw materials from other lands, used them to make products, and then began to sell those products back to other countries.

Asian countries, up to a certain period, did not have to worry as much about food, so they lived fairly peacefully. But then the imperialists came, and they lived under imperial rule, which became an obstacle to their development.

Eventually part of the population in Asia received a Western-style education, adopted a Western way of thinking, and imported Western technologies, which led to trade with Western countries.

In Asian countries, business had existed on a local level, but European colonization allowed it to expand to an international level. In Asian countries, one part of the population adopted Western ways of doing things and became rich, while those who still followed an ancient way of life remained poor.

At a global level, the standard of living in industrialized nations rose to a much higher level than that of the exploited nations, and these nations became much more economically powerful.

In those exploited nations, the few individuals who had the opportunity to adopt a Western way of life became wealthy, while peasants and villagers who preserved the same lifestyle they had for thousands of years remained poor.

Exploitation is an interesting word. I have just described material exploitation.

But I am also an exploiter. I hold the position of a high monk, a big lama. Unless I exercise self-restraint, there is every possibility for me to exploit others.

On my first visit to Mongolia, they arranged a tour to various institutions and a museum. At the museum, I saw a drawing of a lama with a huge mouth, eating up the people.

This was in 1979, when Mongolia was still a Communist country. The Communists said that religion was a drug, and every religious institution was an exploiter. Even monks were exploiters. Even donations distributed to the monastic community were considered to be a form of exploitation.

When I came to the spot with that picture, the officials were a little bit nervous. I deliberately looked at it and I said, "It's true."

Of course, I agree. I am not only a socialist but also a bit leftist, a communist. In terms of social economy theory, I am a Marxist. I think I am farther to the left than the Chinese leaders. [Bursts out laughing.] They are capitalists. [Laughs again.]

But this idea of exploitation has brought us full circle in our discussion. We began with this question:

"HOW SHOULD WE DEAL WITH INEQUALITY AND SOCIAL INJUSTICE? IS IT UN-BUDDHIST TO FEEL ANGER?"

"In the real world exploitation exists, and there is a great and unjust gap between rich and poor. The question is, from a Buddhist perspective, how should we deal with inequality and social injustice? Is it un-Buddhist to feel anger and indignation in the midst of such circumstances?"

"I CAN BE ANGRY.

BUT THIS ANGER IS

COMPASSION."

Being Angry

I recently had an audience with a group of refugees that had just arrived in Dharamsala from China.

These were people who had risked their lives to cross the Himalayas, unafraid of the cold or altitude sickness or the danger of getting shot. Many of those who survive such a crossing have to have fingers or toes amputated because of frostbite. Some collapse and fall ill when they arrive.

First they are treated at a refugee receiving center in Nepal, and once they have recovered their strength, they travel in groups of several dozen at a time to Dharamsala. It is there that I met with them.

This was an overwhelming moment for the refugee people who had just arrived. They were trembling with emotion. Yet behind that emotion there was surely great sadness. Who would go into exile if he were happy?

Their families had been killed and tortured; they had faced poverty and despair. Sustained only by the hope of exile, they had to risk their lives to cross the border.

I too am in exile. I know their sadness. I know their suffering. I felt their sadness and pain, all the absurdity and cruelty they had encountered.

"I CAN EXPERIENCE THE SADNESS, SUFFERING, THE ABSURDITY, AND CRUELTY OF THIS WORLD. I CAN SHARE IN OTHERS' PAIN. I FEEL THE SAME ANGER AND OUTRAGE."

"THAT ANGER MOTIVATES ME TO WORK HARDER IN MY OWN RELIGIOUS PRACTICE, SO THAT I CAN CONFRONT THAT SUFFERING DIRECTLY AND ENLIGHTEN HUMANITY."

But here I now sit, and I can laugh heartily and speak freely.

This is not an emotional switch I turn on and off. That meeting and this moment are connected. I can experience the sadness, suffering, the absurdity, and cruelty of this world. I can share in others' pain and groan with them. I feel the same anger and outrage.

But in the present moment, that anger motivates me to find the causes of suffering in the world and to work harder in my own religious practice, so that I can confront that suffering directly and enlighten humanity.

I do this so that, without exploiting myself or those refugees or resorting to violence, I can help create a society that will bring freedom and happiness to all people.

I can be angry.

But this anger is compassion. The experience of pain and sorrow leads to enlightenment and a deep wish for salvation.

A great desire for freedom emerges. To go from pain to limitless freedom is Buddhism.

That is the path the Buddha himself took.

Hampton Roads Publishing Company

. . . for the evolving human spirit

Hampton Roads Publishing Company publishes books on a variety of subjects, including spirituality, health, and other related topics.

For a copy of our latest trade catalog, call (978) 465-0504 or visit our distributor's website at *www.redwheelweiser.com*. You can also sign up for our newsletter and special offers by going to *www.redwheelweiser.com/newsletter.*